SELF-CONTROL

by Henrietta Gambill

illustrated by Kathryn Hutton

Distributed by Childrens Press, 1224 West Van Buren Street,
Chicago, Illinois 60607

Library of Congress Cataloging in Publication Data

Gambill, Henrietta, 1927-
  Self-control.

  (What is it?)
  Summary: Offers advice for young children on
how to use self-control in their lives.
   1. Self-control—Moral and ethical aspects—
Juvenile literature.   [1. Self-control]
I. Hutton, Kathryn, ill.   II. Title.
III. Series.
BJ1533.D49G35 1982   179'.9   82-1201
ISBN 0-89565-225-0   AACR2

Self-control is a good thing to have. But how do you get it? What is self-control?

Self-control is listening to your
friend talk when you want him to
listen to you!

Letting someone else take the biggest
piece of candy takes self-control.

And waiting until after dinner to eat
your piece takes even more!

Letting your cat down to play when
she wiggles takes self-control, because
it's such fun to hold her close and
listen to her purr.

Not laughing when your sister falls
down—that takes LOTS of self-control.

When your brother punches you for no good reason (except, maybe, that you've been teasing him), do you punch him back as hard as you can?

Not if you have self-control!

When your baby sister is asleep and you want to play with her but, instead, you tiptoe quietly out, that's having self-control.

And self-control is not feeding the dog
when he begs at the table.

When your team loses because you
struck out,

self-control keeps you from throwing
your bat down.

17

Being quiet in the library takes self-control, especially when a friend comes in and you want to call to him.

QUIET,
PLEASE

Self-control is lining up when the
teacher asks you to—and not pushing
the person in front of you!

Self-control is waiting for the scissors—without complaining—when you and a friend are sharing a pair.

And when you don't know the answers, self-control is keeping your eyes on your own paper.

Self-control is listening quietly when
Teacher tells a story.

Waiting for your mom and dad, without complaining, takes lots of self-control.

Self-control means you really think
and decide what is right for you to do.

Having self-control will help you to be
a happy person.